Forty

The Evolution of a Collection

Written by Heather Audin

The
Quilters' Guild

The Quilters' Guild of the British Isles is the national organisation for people involved in patchwork and quilting; it has over 7000 members.

ISBN 978-0-9564789-3-1

Published by The Quilters' Guild of the British Isles

www.quiltersguild.org.uk

The Quilters' Guild is registered in England & Wales as a company limited by guarantee no. 03447631 and as a charity no. 1067361 and as a charity in Scotland no. SC043174. Registered office: St Anthony's Hall, Peasholme Green, York YO1 7PW. Tel: 01904 613242. Festival of Quilts Ltd (trading as QGBI Enterprises) is a company limited by guarantee, reg. no. 3538705

Contents

Sponsors

The Quilters' Guild is very grateful to all our sponsors
for their support in the production of this publication.

representing:

President's Foreword

I am delighted to welcome you to *Forty; The Evolution of a Collection* which celebrates the 40th birthday of The Quilters' Guild of the British Isles in 2019, our Ruby anniversary year.

Forty features a selection of the quilts that have been added to our Collection during each decade of the life of The Quilters' Guild. In featuring these quilts, we are able to share with you not just 40 years of collecting but also the breadth of our British quilting heritage and the work of quilters, both past and present.

The Guild is grateful to all those who have been involved in developing what has become an internationally significant collection. From the enthusiasm and foresight of our early volunteers working in their own homes to the present day, where volunteers and staff work together, the constant factor has been a remarkable level of dedication and professionalism that has served The Guild well.

Whilst we look forward to the next decade with its opportunities for adding to The Collection, increasing our knowledge and making our Collection as widely available as possible, I hope you enjoy this reflection on the first 40 years of quilt collecting.

Linda Bilsborrow
President, The Quilters' Guild of the British Isles

Introduction

This book celebrates the 40th anniversary of The Quilters' Guild Museum Collection, a dedicated textile collection of over 850 examples of British patchwork, quilting and appliqué that range in date from the early eighteenth century until 2018.

The Collection has grown steadily since the formation of The Quilters' Guild in 1979, and thanks to the determined efforts of knowledgeable Quilters' Guild volunteers and staff it forms a rich and valuable resource that represents an interesting and important part of the social and domestic history of Britain over the last three centuries.

No collection, regardless of size or origin, springs into being, but rather is the result of gradual development and varying speeds of growth. Over the last four decades our collecting priorities have changed, as The Collection grew larger and scholarship on the history of patchwork and quilting increased. In the early years most items were accepted regardless of style, composition and condition, but as The Collection grew, periodic assessments were important to identify gaps and to rationalise

any duplication, keeping it relevant, focused, and our resources efficiently used. Currently, a Collections Committee contributes a variety of skills and expertise to decide on new acquisitions, and a collections policy ensures everyone follows the same guidelines, identifying what we can and can't accept, and outlining important areas for expansion.

This book explores 40 years of collecting through 40 different objects, which have been divided into four sections – one for each decade of the life of The Guild. Each section charts some of the key events in relation to the evolution of The Collection and its accessibility to the public, starting with a few objects intended for the education of Guild members to a large specialist collection accessible for the benefit of anyone interested in the history of patchwork and quilting.

As with any publication, there are limitations. This book is not all-encompassing, but rather a snapshot through the decades aimed at providing the reader with an impression of the variety and breadth of our Collection. Deciding on which items should feature in the book was a difficult and daunting task! We could easily have chosen any item in The Collection to represent our collecting activity over the last 40 years. Each has a deserving place and represents something important from our patchwork and quilting heritage. Those who know The Collection well will undoubtedly have come across some of these items before, or indeed may find that their favourite item is missing. This is not a reflection on its perceived importance or status – there were just so many items to choose from and only a small proportion from each decade could be included. Nor is there a hierarchy – everything is important for different reasons, each as equally valid as the next.

This book is also not a comprehensive history of The Quilters' Guild – that has yet to be written. Of course, The Collection does not exist in isolation, and key events in The Guild's history that are related to The Collection are covered in the introduction to each decade. But it is recognised that there is much more to be said about The Guild and all of its dedicated members and champions who have been involved over the last 40 years, and who have made it the organisation that it is today.

Early Years: 1979–1989

"It is felt by many quiltmakers throughout the country…that a strong, well run organisation is now needed to bring quiltmakers into closer contact with each other, to better the skills of the individual and promote the Art of Quiltmaking in this country. It is proposed therefore that we should form a Quiltmakers Guild."

Extract from archives of The Quilters' Guild.

Frances Anne Kemble with the House Blocks Quilt at the first AGM, 1980

In August 1979, approximately 40 people gathered in an upstairs room of The British Crafts Centre (later Contemporary Applied Arts) in Covent Garden, and unanimously agreed to form a Guild of Quiltmakers. An initial steering committee would oversee the establishment of a quarterly newsletter, the encouragement of a regional network, and the first exhibition and AGM. With founder membership priced £6, The Quilters' Guild (the name formally decided on) had just over 800 members by the end of its first year. Local groups were growing and the message was spreading – the latest revival and interest in patchwork and quilting looked set to continue its upward surge.

In the decade leading up to the establishment of The Quilters' Guild, the popularity of the crafts had been growing steadily. Two major American quilt exhibitions are often cited as landmark events that introduced a different style of quilting to British quiltmakers. These were the touring American pieced quilts from the collection of Jonathan Holstein and Gail Van der Hoof, previously on show at the Renwick Gallery of the National Collection of Fine Arts in Washington, which travelled to two venues in Britain in 1975; and a selection of quilts from The American Museum in Britain displayed at the Commonwealth Institute in 1976. The more traditional hexagon

The Quilters' Guild steering committee 1979

patchwork was also experiencing something of a renaissance. The National Federation of Women's Institutes patchwork exhibition at Sanderson House in 1970 saw in excess of a staggering 800 entries, with hexagon mosaic patchwork predominating.

The Guild itself was a response to rather than a creator of the revival, and certainly there were patchwork and quilting groups that existed before The Guild was formed. The Quilt Circle newsletter, published from 1978, was instrumental in bringing people together, providing organised quilting events and enabling contact and the exchange of ideas.

When this venture began to flounder, many of its members understood the importance of this strong connection between quilters for the encouragement and development of the craft, and were amongst the majority of the attendees at that very first meeting forming The Quilters' Guild in 1979.

From its inception, The Guild had always realised the importance of creating a collection – to inspire and educate its members and to preserve the history of the allied crafts of patchwork and quilting, at that time both relatively unexplored within the realm of social and domestic history. Certainly their

Attendees of the first AGM, Winchester, 1980

foresight in doing this has led to the creation of an internationally significant, dedicated collection, which can be researched, viewed and exhibited for the benefit of not just Guild members, but anyone interested in the crafts for generations to come.

The first decade can be viewed as The Collection finding its feet, before the parameters and focus were fine-tuned in later decades. This is to be expected – The Guild itself was a new organisation, and they were grateful for any and all examples that aided their educational goals. Although there were only 36 pieces collected in the first 10 years, The Collection was already showing great variety, including wholecloths, mosaic patchwork, crazy patchwork and frame pieces spanning the early nineteenth century to 1979. Some of those early pieces were actually American in origin, and have since found more appropriate homes in other collections, including The American Museum in Britain, Bath.

Front cover of the first *Newsletter*, Winter 1979

Founder member membership card

As The Collection became larger and more focused, it was later decided that its remit should match the British-wide focus of the organisation itself.

Initially, progress was slow and unplanned, which was probably just as well. With no central headquarters or repository to store the quilts, they were kept in members' houses and cared for by dedicated volunteers, who catalogued them, packed them and prepared them for any exhibitions. The first *Newsletter* in Winter of 1979 anticipated that it could take a while to find a storehouse, stating: 'It may be some time before a home can be found for The Collection; meanwhile it will be displayed whenever possible – probably for the first time at the first annual general meeting early in 1980.' Collections-related activity, like the rest of The Guild, relied solely on voluntary support. Meanwhile The Quilters' Guild itself continued to grow, to attract new members, and to explore interesting debates and ideas around the evolving and re-emerging crafts.

The House Blocks Quilt

Made 1978–1979 | 188cm x 236cm | Acquired in 1979

This quilt was the first acquisition into The Collection of the newly formed Quilters' Guild. The blocks were actually the prize for a quilt competition set by The Quilt Circle in the summer of 1979. The idea for the blocks was inspired by Cambridge Quilters, who had combined with an American quilt group to make house blocks for an international exchange. Each of the 20 different appliqué house blocks is unique to the individual makers, made to represent their actual personal residence or a typical house style in the area where the maker lived. The quilt competition was won by Jean Amsden, but the house blocks – which were the prize – were handed over unfinished. Jean framed the pieces and with the help of her daughter Deirdre assembled the blocks, added the wadding and bound the edge. With the formation of The Guild in 1979, many members of The Quilt Circle became members of The Guild, and so it was fitting that the first acquisition represented their work.

Maureen Thomas's house block

The quilt was exhibited at the first Quilters' Guild AGM in April 1980, which was held at King Alfred's College in Winchester. It was noted in the very first *Newsletter* in 1979 that 'It may be some time before a home can be found for the collection; meanwhile it will be displayed whenever possible'. Even with just one item, the commitment to both creating and displaying a collection was already clear.

Deirdre Amsden's house block

Both Jean and Deirdre played important roles throughout the history of The Quilters' Guild. Deirdre was the first president of The Quilters' Guild, from 1979 to 1982. She is known for her pioneering colourwash technique, which graduates carefully selected tones of printed cotton fabrics to create a new piece of cloth, and several pieces of her work are present in The Collection. Jean was the first editor of The Quilters' Guild *Newsletter* as well as an active teacher, maker and Guild member. She has work in the Nineties Collection and was also the maker of what has become one of the most popular and perhaps most unusual patchwork items in The Collection – a patchwork bikini made from Sanderson furnishing fabrics in the 1970s!

Claridge's Peach Wholecloth Quilt

Made in the 1930s | 196cm x 226cm | Acquired in 1980

Carefully designed and skilfully sewn, this peach and blue cotton wholecloth represents a period of quiltmaking in the twentieth century when it was feared the craft was in decline and in danger of being lost altogether. The interwar years were difficult times for traditional crafts. Quilting, especially the wholecloth style, lost popularity and skilful practitioners, and faced competition from commercial alternatives that were more fashionable, cheap and easily available. Younger generations had different lifestyles and weren't necessarily taught the same traditional skills as their mothers and grandmothers.

In an attempt to prevent these crafts from dying out altogether, the Rural Industries Bureau was established in the late 1920s. Workshops and classes were set up in the North Country and Wales, which concentrated on using current quilters to teach skills to younger generations whilst fulfilling orders for quilted products to high-class clients, creating work of the highest quality. Items were sold through fashionable London outlets such as Muriel Rose's Little Gallery. The benefit of this also extended to the quilters themselves, providing an income to quilters and their families in the poorest areas.

This particular piece is one of two donated to The Collection at the same time. It features traditional Welsh motifs including beech leaves, spirals and roses. Clare Claridge has noted that inside some of the small circles, disguised as a spiral, is the letter 'C' – which stands for Cymru (Wales). This was the signature mark of the Abertridwr group. Both this, and a grey quilt, were commissioned by the fashionable Claridge's Hotel in London, for their newly refurbished Art Deco wing which opened in 1932. In a change of fortune, a traditional form of quilting that was originally regarded as quite ordinary, created in rural areas for warmth and comfort, was now highly prized for the fashionable elite and commanded a significant price. It was also important as a form of social responsibility, making a significant difference to the lives of the poorer classes who otherwise had few means of making a living.

A blue fabric was used for the reverse of the quilt

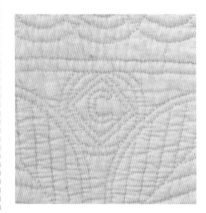

Quilted 'C' for Cymru (Wales)

Avril's signature style: skilful fussy-cutting and arrangement

Fussy-cut miniature pin cushion

Hexagon patches on a very small scale

Averil Colby Samples

Made 1950s–1980s | Various sizes | Acquired in 1983

By the time of The Quilters' Guild formation in 1979, Averil Colby's importance as a practitioner and historical researcher of patchwork and quilting was well known. She accepted The Guild's invitation to become their first honorary member, and an interesting article on her in the winter *Newsletter* in 1979 displayed her forthright views and personality. Colby was the first person to really research and publish comprehensively on the subjects, giving them emphasis as worthy aspects of social history rather than unimportant domestic textiles. Her own practice concentrated on the mosaic patchwork method, and her use of carefully selected fussy-cut shapes arranged to create new designs became her signature style. Some of her work was in a minuscule scale, as can be seen by several of the unfinished samples.

Some of the views she expressed are today considered old-fashioned, and don't encompass the variety of styles and creativity apparent in contemporary quiltmaking. She firmly believed that the true basis of patchwork was thrift, using up old scraps and offcuts rather than buying new; that machines should only be used if they could be executed as skilfully as a hand needle; and that all patchwork and quilting should be made practically for use. She believed anything too far removed from its traditional base becomes something different entirely. Whilst all individual views are valid, the growth in contemporary practice and quilters pushing the boundaries of quiltmaking over the next few decades would show an interesting evolution of what was considered a quilt, and how quilting could be used as a valid form of artistic expression.

These samples and fabrics were donated to The Quilters' Guild after the death of Averil Colby in 1983. Her extensive fabric collection included a large range of historic printed cottons which are useful for dating the patchwork pieces within our heritage quilt collection. Colby used many historic fabrics in her patchwork creations – leaving small hexagon-shaped holes spread out over the surface where a favoured fussy-cut flower was required to complete her desired design.

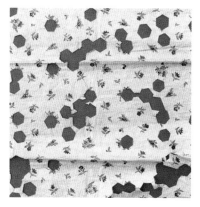

Hexagon-shaped holes left from fussy cutting

Averil standing by her dresser

Baby Blocks Coverlet

Made in the 1890s | 198cm x 221cm | Acquired in 1987

This stunning coverlet embodies the heavily over-furnished late Victorian fancywork style and uses both mosaic and crazy patchwork which is further framed by a heavy passementerie edging often found on upholstery. The velvets and silks are fashionable and not in the slightest bit practical, aiming to demonstrate the wealth and status of the maker, who can afford expensive fabrics and the time taken to create such a time-consuming object. The artificial dyes used to create the vibrant array of colours give the patchwork a jewel-like quality. It's a little busy on the eye, but a perfect testament to the fashionable parlour of the Victorian age.

The patchwork styles and age of this piece are not in themselves rare. In fact, late Victorian patchworks account for a good number of items offered to The Guild over the past 40 years, but this one has several factors in its favour that make it an important acquisition for The Collection. The condition is good, which can be rare for late nineteenth-century silks. As well as being a fragile natural fabric prone to pest attack, their dyeing and manufacturing processes often mean that Victorian silks deteriorate, even if they have never actually been used. This piece also has provenance, that rare information: images that tell us who made it, where they made it and when, and in this case where some of the fabrics may have come from. As a piece of social history, there is nothing more interesting than knowing about the people behind the objects.

We know that this coverlet was made by Catherine Issell Briggs (née Jarvis), born in Devonshire in 1856 and apprenticed aged 14 to a dressmaker. She married John Vernon Briggs in Chelsea in 1881, then worked with her husband in their upholstery and furnishing business. It is thought the wide range of fabrics could have been spare pieces from her business, and the bobble fringing was given to her by one of their suppliers, the Holdsworth Brothers.

The placement of colours creates a three dimensional impression

Bobble fringe edging from the Holdsworth Brothers

Catherine with her husband John Briggs

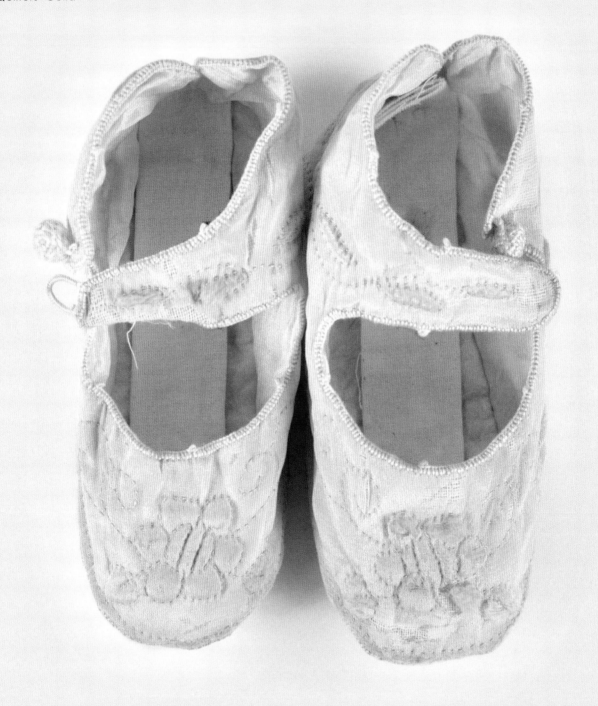

Baby Slippers

Made in the 1930s | Each slipper measures 11.5cm x 5cm |
Acquired in 1988

These delicate slippers are one of the smallest items in The Collection, and feature dainty pink flowers and green leaves, with tiny alternate green and pink leaves along the cross-bar which is fastened by a small loop and button. They were made by hand using the shadow quilting technique. This uses brightly coloured wool to provide texture to the quilted design, which is muted to a gentler colour due to the finer, less opaque material used for the top layer. Shadow quilting was popular, particularly in the interwar years, but then rarely stitched outside that time. Projects featuring this method of quilting could be found in magazines, which gave patterns and designs for various other domestic and clothing items such as dressing gowns and lingerie cases.

It is unlikely that these slippers were ever worn and are more a keepsake than a practical item. Due to the nature of the delicate fabrics used in the top layer, shadow-quilted items don't always stand the test of time and are especially vulnerable where the high relief of the internal stuffing puts pressure and wear on the fabric. It does, however, allow a glimpse of the bright internal coloured wools in contrast to the pastel tones of the intended finished look.

Pink wool can be seen where the fabric has disintegrated

Decorative basket weave design

Godstone Grannies Hexagon Coverlet

Made 1960–1965 | 189cm x 252cm | Acquired in 1989

This piece is undeniably a product of its time. The diamond arrangement of the yellow and brown printed cottons provides a striking design that has a classic 'retro' appeal to more contemporary audiences. Whilst on the surface it may appear to be just another hexagons patchwork, it must be remembered that it was made before the general mass quilting revival in the next decade, and therefore represents the style of patchwork that was popular at that time. Mosaic patchwork hexagons were almost synonymous with the word patchwork in general, with little variation or guidance before the revival provided a wider range of learning opportunities and potential designs to branch out to. This follows in the Averil Colby tradition and is significant as it was made by a Women's Institute group, where Colby's influence as a member and teacher was centred.

This particular coverlet was made for the Surrey Room at Denman College, the Women's Institute residential college where courses, including patchwork, were taught. The project was led by Mollie Simmonds, and a group of members of several different Women's Institutes met at her house in Godstone to stitch the hexagons into diamond shapes, before assembling the whole piece. The materials were largely supplied by dressmaking friends, a common source of fabric before the proliferation of specific patchwork cottons that quilters are used to today.

The diamond arrangements vary across the piece

Fussy-cut floral designs

A Growing Collection: 1990–1999

The nineties saw a rapid expansion of The Collection, and a definite recognition of the importance of our patchwork and quilting heritage – the need to record it, collect it and research it. A large number of key and iconic acquisitions were collected during this decade, and many have become recognisable items to those familiar with The Collection. But this decade was not exclusively historical in its collecting focus. For the first time The Guild began to think about contemporary collecting, recognising the need to capture current quiltmaking practice and commissioning contemporary makers to represent the crafts of patchwork and quilting in the present.

The British Quilt Heritage Project was launched in 1990, and took place in 29 different locations across the UK. The aim of the project was to create a national index of privately owned quilts, coverlets and items

Textile expert Deryn O'Connor (left, in red) assesses a quilt at the Basingstoke Documentation Day

made before 1960, recording the rich heritage and variety of patchwork and quilting in people's homes across the nation. The reasons for the project were twofold: to record the artistic skill and historic character of quiltmakers from all social backgrounds; and to raise awareness and appreciation of this part of our textile heritage so that families knew how to cherish and care for the family heirlooms in their possession. Members of the public had their quilts appraised and photographed, and access to expertise on fabrics, construction and quilting history made the project an overwhelming success, recording over 4000 quilts in a three-year period. It was made possible by a dedicated team of highly knowledgeable, skilled and enthusiastic Quilters' Guild volunteers, generous financial donations and unbelievable organisational support.

The culmination of the collected data and subsequent research was the publication of *Quilt Treasures* in 1995, a comprehensive record of quiltmaking in Britain. Chapters written by leading authorities on quilts, quilting, textiles and quilt care made it an important contribution to the study of quilt history. By raising public awareness of The Quilters' Guild and their educational aims, some of

The Kiss, Siripan Kidd, 62cm x 63cm, 1997

the items examined during the Documentation Days were subsequently donated to The Collection. Items recorded during the British Quilt Heritage Project, and those featured in *Quilt Treasures*, continue to be offered to The Collection nearly three decades after the project began.

This decade also saw the establishment of The British Quilt Study Group in 1998, the first of The Quilters' Guild specialist groups. Open to researchers, enthusiasts, quilt lovers and collectors, the focus of this group is not on making new pieces, but rather on examining and researching those already made. Whilst many of its members are fascinated by the historical subjects for research, the aims of the group are to encourage interest and study of historical and contemporary pieces, and several of its members have been instrumental in producing research and papers on contemporary practice. Annual seminars feature presentations of members'

Quilt Treasures, first published 1995

research which is then published in *Quilt Studies*, celebrating its 20th volume in 2019. Many of these papers have researched items in The Collection, providing a significant body of knowledge that is useful for exhibition interpretation and educational activities for the benefit of the public.

The Nineties Collection was another major achievement during this decade, and provided a body of contemporary work which brought The Collection right up to date in representing the developments of the quilting world. A distinct collection within the main Collection, compiling these pieces was a decade-long process, as they were commissioned by the Regions of The Guild from local makers. Pieces showcase a variety of styles and techniques, and the Nineties Collection provided a foundation for collecting contemporary work which has since been expanded as the decades have progressed.

Both the Nineties Collection and the Heritage Collection were exhibited at 27 venues between 1995 and 1999, including several exhibitions at the Bankfield Museum in Halifax, the Harris Museum and Art Gallery in Preston, The Shipley Art Gallery in Newcastle, and a display at the first ever Festival of Quilts at Lord's Cricket Ground in London in 1999, in The Guild's 20th anniversary year. Curator Mary Ranby and her assistants were always keen to display new acquisitions, and worked hard to ensure that Collection items on show were rotated to give visitors something new to see.

As it entered the millennium, the size of The Collection had grown from 36 to over 350 pieces – a remarkable achievement but one in desperate need of re-housing. It had outgrown the existing arrangement of being held in members' houses, and needed a centralised home where it could be more easily accessed and cared for.

Return Flight, Anja Townrow, 61cm x 60.2cm, 1999

Tyneside Signature Quilt

Made in 1897 | 222cm x 222cm | Acquired in 1990

This community fundraising quilt had a dual purpose: to commemorate Queen Victoria's Diamond Jubilee in 1897, and to raise much needed funds for the local church. It features red, pale blue and white hand-embroidered signatures on a white cotton quilted background, which surround an embroidered outline of Queen Victoria's head in the centre. The inscription above her head reads 'Primitive Methodist Connexion Jarrow on Tyne Circuit' and underneath '1837 Diamond Jubilee 1897'. Signature quilts raised funds by participants paying to have their name embroidered on a square. In some cases, they wrote their name themselves (sometimes specified as autograph quilts), and in others it would be written for them in the same neat hand. The finished quilt would often also be raffled, raising further money for the chosen cause.

It was made by the women of Ellison Street Methodist Church, a 'Cathedral church' in Jarrow, South Tyneside. Research by Anne Jeater suggests that the 212 sponsors were largely class leaders and other church officers, and the more affluent members of the congregation and their families. The majority of the 'ordinary' membership would not have been able to afford even the few pence needed to sponsor a square. Circuit ministers and their families, as well as prominent names in the congregation, can all be found closest to the centre of the quilt, indicating their position within the community. These include Robert Reavley ('Mineral Water Manufacturer') and Thomas Taylor Harvey ('Rolling Mill Manager & Circuit Steward').

Signature quilts are a valuable snapshot of a community at a specified time and place, doing a particular activity. Their fundraising nature often means the activity is further recorded in local newspapers or church records. The minutes of the Ellison Street Trustees Meeting in 1898 record simply 'Moved and carried that the money Mrs Odlum obtained for autograph quilt go to purchase carpet for the Rostrum and likewise curtains for the front of the organ. Mrs Harvey & Reavley to attend it'. Based on the average cost of carpet in 1897 and the area of the Rostrum, it is estimated that the quilt raised £12–£20, which is the equivalent to £1000–£1800 today.

Signatures in various handwriting and embroidery styles

Signature of Robert Reavley, 'Mineral Water Manufacturer'

Mrs Fitzherbert Top

Made 1800–1850 | 230cm x 280cm | Acquired in 1991

There are several interesting and unusual elements to this pieced top that make it more than a visually striking patchwork. The majority of the silk pieces are ribbons, and their neat selvedge edges can be seen when the single-layer top is viewed from the back. The earliest ribbons date to the first decades of the nineteenth century, the latest to around the middle of that century. The array of colours and patterns in the silks adds to the mesmerising effect of the zigzags and prairie point triangles. This is a bold piece, yet its delicate fabrics make it soft and light. Its large size, fragile nature and lack of backing mean it is a difficult piece to exhibit but it is the kind of textile that can only be truly appreciated in person.

Additional centre piece not attached to the main top

The first conundrum relating to this piece is its additional centre. When it was acquired, a new centre had been placed over the top, with bold stripes to match the outer borders. However, a more delicate, pieced white centre remained, undamaged, underneath. Why was the new piece created to cover the centre? Did the maker change her mind on her fabric choice, or was it made to protect the original centre? These central white pieces are the ones thought to be the oldest.

The second is its link to some more unusual provenance – the type that is very exciting but also highly tenuous, without real validation and impossible to prove either for or against! The central square is supposed to contain fabric from the wedding dress of Mrs Fitzherbert, the Catholic and twice widowed mistress of George IV. She married George, in secret and without royal approval, in 1785. It is unclear where this story has come from, as it is recorded in the object file as being given at the time of acquisition. It's a wonderful story, but we have no way of knowing if any part of it is true – another element of this patchwork that will remain a mystery.

Colourful silk ribbons show the variety of designs available

Cigarette Silks Tea Cosy

Made in the 1920s | 35cm x 27.5cm | Acquired in 1992

There are a number of patchwork and quilted tea cosies in The Collection that vary in style and date from late Victorian embroidered splendour to mid-twentieth-century printed hexagons. This one is of particular interest and demonstrates the novelty of collecting and the effectiveness of marketing. It is made from printed B.D.V.[1] cigarette silks, which have been joined together and decorated along the seams with feather stitch in different-coloured embroidery threads. One side features the 'Old Masters' paintings set whilst the other shows a collection of birds. A delicate multicoloured ruffled silk strip adorns the edge, although this has deteriorated and is now protected by a layer of conservation netting.

The reverse side of the tea cosy

Cigarette silks were decorative and colourful collectable items issued by manufacturers to encourage customer brand loyalty. They were marketed towards women, and although it was just starting to be socially acceptable for women to be smokers, it was also believed that women would put pressure on their male family members to purchase a certain brand of cigarettes so that she could collect the full set of silks for her domestic projects. Coupons were sent away and the fabrics would arrive, destined to be used in patchwork coverlets, samplers, bags and, as in this case, tea cosies. Various series were devised, including flags, political figures, county coats of arms and even ceramics. This style of printed cigarette silks was no longer produced by the late 1920s, and they were replaced with a woven equivalent, which was itself then replaced by printed cigarette cards.

Detail of the 'Old Masters' series

An example of a short-lived fashionable phase, this tea cosy represents an interesting interplay between the commercial world, family life and a product intended for men, but marketed towards women with an understanding of how buying power and pressure was firmly within the female realm.

1   B.D.V. was a popular brand of cigarettes available from the early 1900s to 1948.

The Jubilee Quilt

Made in 1887 | 204cm x 202cm | Acquired in 1992

There can be no greater celebratory quilt than this marvellous compendium of complex construction, creative embroidery and accomplished technique. Made to celebrate Queen Victoria's Golden Jubilee in 1887, the log cabin flower petals surround a three-dimensional central pistil and are presumed to represent chrysanthemums, whose name means 'golden flower' in Greek. Charming pictorial references to Victorian life are illustrated in the patchwork fans on the outer border, with embroidered children, fashionable ladies, soldiers and policemen – each with a different collar identity number. In fact, there is so much embroidery and decoration that this wondrous piece teeters dangerously on the brink of being over-embellished, dividing opinion and often attracting the contradictory exclamation of absolute awe coupled with 'I couldn't have it in my house!'

The extent to which it was used is debatable as it survives in near perfect condition, and it has been suggested that this was more of an exhibition piece than a functional object. It was made by Ann Mills of Crook in County Durham, who lived near the main high street of the town with her husband, Thomas Mills, and her mother-in-law Lydia. Thomas was a tailor and draper, working from his home in Commercial Street, and it is thought that some of the strips of fabric could have been remnants from his work. Such a time-consuming and decorative piece must surely have been highly treasured, but what we do know is that it didn't stay with the Mills family for very long. At some point after its completion the family fell on hard times and were unable to pay the rent on their house. This quilt was given to their landlord, William Machell, in lieu of rent. It was then handed down through Machell's family before being recorded at a British Quilt Heritage Project Documentation Day and subsequently donated to The Quilters' Guild Collection in 1992.

Fans on the outer border feature intricate embroidered figures

An embroidered Queen Victoria features in the centre of each corner flower

Miniature four-poster bed and squares quilt by Barbara Bailey

Barbara with one of her pet ducks, Olympia

Barbara with the grapes grown in her garden

Barbara Bailey Miniature Quilts

Made in the 1970s–1980s | Various sizes | Acquired in 1993

There are 20 miniature quilts made by Barbara Bailey in The Collection, varying in style from simple quilted pieces outlining the front printed cotton design, to more intricate miniature log cabin and paper pieced techniques. They were made to fit two different miniature beds, one a wooden rocking cradle with heart-shaped head and foot boards, and the other a four-poster bed complete with curtains and tester hangings. The beds and the quilts were intended to be featured in Averil Colby's publication on miniature pieces, and were photographed ready for what would have been her sixth publication. Unfortunately, Colby died before it was finished and the book was never published.

The miniature pieces are part of a larger Barbara Bailey Collection which features full-size quilts and coverlets, items of clothing, teaching samples, and an abundance of photographs and slides that document her main passions – patchwork, gardening and travelling. Both Barbara and her sister Dulcie were keen practitioners, teachers and founder members of The Quilters' Guild. They also founded their own local group, The Garth and Wraxall Quilters, in 1974 which met regularly at their small bungalow overlooking the Somerset Levels. Their shared home was filled with their creations, and every year their rooms were further filled with an exhibition showcasing their group's work. Both sisters were keen gardeners and cultivated a spectacular garden of unusual plants which was home to their pet duck Olympia. Barbara was also known for her eccentric dress sense, often wearing her patchwork creations, including a large green appliqué cape made during a Guild workshop that she wore to The Quilters' Guild AGM in 1984.

Barbara's generosity, love of patchwork and involvement in The Quilters' Guild can be seen by the large bequest she left on her in death in 1993. This money was used to help look for a home for The Guild and The Collection and enabled the move to the current headquarters at St Anthony's Hall in York, where the Quilt Museum was opened in 2008. The Bailey Gallery was named after her in honour of her role in The Guild and her generous bequest.

Miniature log cabin quilt by Barbara Bailey

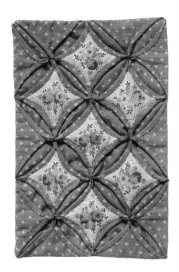

Miniature cathedral windows quilt by Barbara Bailey

Mariner's Compass Coverlet

Made in the 1820s by Mary Dennis | 252cm x 273cm | Acquired in 1994

This vibrant coverlet is exquisitely constructed with a precision-pieced pointed compass centre and demonstrates the wide range of beautiful printed designs available on cottons from the first decades of the nineteenth century. It has well recorded provenance and is one of five items made by the same family that were all donated at the same time. It is fortunate that the family kept photographs and *carte de visite* portraits, as these help those who view the coverlet today to imagine the makers and their lives, which span the whole of the Victorian period.

The skilled maker of this piece was Mary Dennis, who most likely made it as part of her 'bottom drawer' in preparation for her marriage to Richard Cann, a Devonshire farmer, in 1828. Mary and Richard had six daughters – Annie, Jane, Elizabeth, Fanny, Mary and Margaret – and one son, John. Unfortunately, Jane died of typhoid fever in 1842, with Richard dying later that same year, leaving Mary and her children no choice but to leave their farm and move to Hartland village where they ran a draper's and grocer's shop. It is presumed that many of the fabrics in the later quilts and coverlets used remnants and offcuts from their drapery business, and with four daughters staying at home to help run the shop it is possible that they all had a hand in making the patchwork that survives today. Only one daughter, Mary, married, and it is presumed that the two cot quilts were made for her only son, Charles Tottenham. Mary Cann and her daughters stayed running the shop for the next 50 years until her death at the age of 92 in 1891.

This piece is important for its construction, range of fabrics and its detailed provenance, which has enabled us to use family history records to build a fuller picture of the makers' lives. It was chosen by Australian designer Karon Styles as the inspiration for a Marcus Fabrics range of reproduction cotton prints in 2016, entitled 'Elizabeth's Dowry', which was extended further with the additional 'Devon County' complementary fabric range in 2017. The first range included a printed central compass panel, allowing quilters to recreate the original without having to piece the compass medallion.

Charles Tottenham, Mary's grandson, outside the Cann & Co. drapery shop

Mary Cann (née Dennis)

The range of different printed cottons used in the coverlet

35

The Billings Coverlet

Made 1805–1810 | 215cm x 215cm | Acquired in 1996

This stunning mosaic patchwork coverlet is a geometric marvel and holds the status of the most technically complex frame design in the whole Collection. Constructed from a vast array of beautiful printed cottons that have been hand pieced over paper templates, each frame has been thoughtfully designed, which can be seen by the way the shapes fit into the corners. Technically this piece is only a top rather than a coverlet and consists of only a single decorative patchwork layer, which was quite common at the time of its construction.

Sadly we don't have much provenance associated with the piece apart from the belief that it was made for a large estate somewhere in Yorkshire. Mrs Billings was the donor rather than the maker, and her enigmatic personality led the cataloguers to name the piece after her. The coverlet was handed down through the family of a housekeeper who worked on the estate, but the quality of the cottons and skill level of its construction and design would point towards a maker of higher social standing, who had the time, education and fabrics to make such a piece. However, even though it was likely to have been made in an affluent household, the fabrics were still a precious resource, and several pieces show where the tiny shapes in this patchwork were joined from even smaller scraps.

The beauty and complexity of this piece has captured the imaginations of many quilters who have recreated their own versions of the coverlet. Its delicate condition means it rarely goes on exhibition, but is carefully preserved as an important resource for researchers.

The corners are masterfully turned with precision

Central frames of the coverlet

Mary Prince Coverlet

Made 1803–1815 by Mary Prince | 230cm x 275cm | Acquired in 1997

The Mary Prince Coverlet is a compendium of late eighteenth and early nineteenth-century printed cottons. The frame design of mosaic patchwork long hexagons is arranged according to colours and tone to provide a visually stunning pattern and demonstrates that the maker was very skilled in both sewing and organising the overall layout. This piece joins several others collected in the 1990s which showcase the expensive fabrics and skilled workmanship of women from a higher social status. They are decorative and lengthy projects, planned and sewn in leisure time rather than practical, utilitarian items made quickly for warmth.

Unusually for an early coverlet, the maker signed this piece in blue cross-stitch embroidery on a piece of linen tape which edges the patchwork and reads 'Mary Prince 1803'. Normally we expect a date to be added at the point of completion, but research undertaken by Deryn O'Connor and Tina Fenwick Smith noted that, in this case, the date was misleading. The central fabrics within the hexagon shape date from a later period as they use a lapis dyeing technique (a process that allowed the printing of madder red directly next to indigo blue without leaving a white gap) that wasn't invented until 1808. Various theories have been suggested, with the favoured idea being that the original centre was somehow damaged, and then replaced with slightly later, more contemporary and fashionable fabrics. The fabric experts also noted that several of the fabrics had three blue threads running through their selvedge, which could be seen from the small seam allowances on the back of the patchwork. These three blue threads were an identification requirement of British manufactured cottons from 1774 to 1811, distinguishing it as exempt from the same strict taxation imposed on imported cottons at that time.

The coverlet's importance as an encyclopaedia of printed cottons has always been recognised, but there were a significant number of fabrics that had deteriorated, making it fragile and difficult to both display and even take out of storage for researchers. In order to preserve it for future generations it was conserved with the aid of a grant from the Association of Independent Museums (AIM) in 2009–2010.

Hexagon rosette before conservation showing typical damage

Hexagon rosette after conservation

Mary Prince embroidery on the reverse of the coverlet

Ladies Work Society

Made 1875–1900 | 256cm x 211cm | Acquired in 1998

The unusual design and origin of this piece makes it an interesting addition to The Collection, and whilst we do not know the specific personal details of the maker, the presence of the Ladies Work Society label on the reverse of the coverlet provides some clues about their life and personal circumstances in the last quarter of the nineteenth century. Made on a background of blue and off-white linen, the appliqué motifs that form the design of this coverlet are of good-quality printed dress fabrics. All of the applied fabric has been couched over its joining edge with embroidery silks, and in the centre of the piece 'Industria' is embroidered in satin stitch. The piece is well made and thoughtfully designed.

The Ladies Work Society was established in 1875 in Sloane Square, London, and provided a respectable means of employment for impoverished gentlewomen. These women needed to earn an income but were restricted by their social position on how they could earn money without also losing their status. The Society provided work and anonymity, whilst capitalising on their particular skill-set of fine needlework. Decoratively embroidered clothing and textiles were made to order through the Society and uncommissioned works were sold through its London premises.

The design of this coverlet shows an influence from the Arts and Crafts movement, which emerged at the end of the nineteenth century. Led by artists such as William Morris, the movement aimed to promote and encourage architecture and the applied arts as worthy artistic disciplines. This particular piece is likely to have been made for an exhibition, as the appliqué design is not a usual one for a domestic commission. Unlike many nineteenth-century pieces, this coverlet could have been designed to have been seen on a wall rather than a bed, which sets it apart within our Collection. It also represents a historical element otherwise unseen: an opportunity provided to a group of women who would otherwise struggle, having fallen through the gap caused by the expectations and limitations of Victorian society. Less visible than more usual records of poverty, these types of philanthropic effort are easily overlooked when material evidence ceases to exist, adding to the importance of this piece within our Collection.

Each appliqué shape is outlined with couching

Decorative embroidery adds further embellishment to the appliqué design

Triple X Wholecloth Quilt

Made 1900–1910 by Nellie Ellison | 226cm x 241cm | Acquired in 1998

This contemporary-looking variation of a wholecloth quilt is thought to have been made by quilt teacher Nellie Ellison in the Castleside area of County Durham in the first decade of the twentieth century. The quilting patterns used to decorate the strips are traditional to the North Country, and include the cable twist, Weardale chain, plait, freehand feathers and scrolling. Although made as a practical bedcover, this quilt has survived in excellent condition, and the presence of original blue pencil markings indicates that it has never been washed.

Wholecloth quilting, where the emphasis is on the quilted design rather than patchwork piecing, was traditional in Wales, the Scottish Borders and the North Country, and each geographical area has its own motifs and layout. In the North Country at this time, professional quilt 'stampers' could be employed to draw quilting designs onto quilt tops sent to them, or they sold ready-made and drawn tops for customers to quilt at home. However, it is possible that as an accomplished quilter and teacher Nellie would have drawn her own pattern rather than sending it away to be marked by another stamper.

We have a large number of wholecloth quilts in The Collection, but the design of this one is different, making it an interesting representation of the variations that were made in what is otherwise a category of quilts with a similar overall appearance, even though the combination of quilting motifs can be individual to the maker. The provenance of the maker also adds to the strength of why this piece is an important addition to The Collection. Interestingly this more unusual design is not entirely unique. Another yellow and white central cross wholecloth quilt was collected in 2010 with the variation of a single rather than triple cross, but it shows that it could have been a popular design.

Professionally 'stamped' quilting design expertly drawn

Two typical North Country motifs

Single cross wholecloth quilt

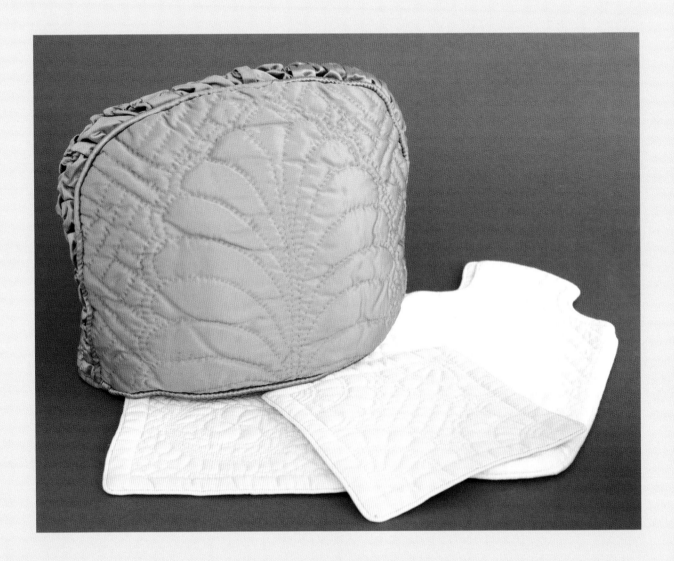

Amy Emms Tea Cosy

Made 1980–1989 by Amy Emms | 35cm x 24cm | Acquired in 1999

This green satin tea cosy with ruched top features a curved feather on one side and a single leaf quilting motif on the other, both with a square diamond background infill. It is one of a number of small items that were donated by the family of Amy Emms, the prominent North Country quilter, on her death in 1998. Also donated were a white hot-water-bottle cover, two pink and blue square quilted coasters and a small selection of tools and chalk from her workbox.

Amy Emms played an integral role in the history of quilting in the twentieth century, helping to keep the traditional craft of North Country quilting alive through teaching and demonstrating at a time when its popularity and practice were in decline. She started quilting very young, helping her mother, threading her needles at the age of 7 and starting to quilt aged 14. Her mother ran a local quilt club, where members would pay a weekly subscription and draw lots to determine the order in which they received their quilt. Her kind and patient manner made her a popular teacher, and her inability to say no meant she always had a long waiting list of commissions, even into her 80s! Her proudest creation was undoubtedly the quilted wedding dress she made for her daughter, Olive, in 1957, which featured in the local *Sunderland Echo*. Her years of quilting, teaching and demonstrating earned her an MBE in 1984 in recognition of her services to the craft.

Amy always advised starting small, on a project like a cushion or a tea cosy, before working up to a bed quilt. This gave the quilter an opportunity to develop their skills, but also to gain a sense of achievement in accomplishing a smaller task, fostering confidence for the next, bigger project. Wholecloth quilts can be daunting, and this advice encouraged development and prevented disillusionment of attempting too big a piece. These small items are therefore very fitting for The Collection, as they represent not only an example of Amy's beautiful quilting, but also of her ethos and personality. She was not ostentatious, but an ordinary North Country woman who was an exceptionally fine quilter.

Gathered detail

Curved feather motif with square diamond infill

45

Going Home, Sheena Norquay, 62cm x 63cm, 1997

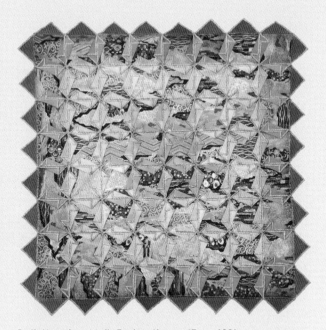

Bath Hanging, Molly Taylor, 61cm x 67cm, 1991

Fish Dance 1, Pauline Burbidge, 60cm x 59cm, 1992

Crazy Craze, Leslie Morgan, 60cm x 60cm, 1997

The Nineties Collection

It was during the second decade of The Collection that the idea of representing contemporary quilting was born. Compiling the Nineties Collection was a decade-long collecting process, which gradually grew as more pieces were donated and commissioned by the Regions of The Quilters' Guild from local quiltmakers and artists.

The intention was to create a distinct contemporary collection that was a snapshot of its period – a body of work to show the best of contemporary quiltmaking at the end of the twentieth century. The Collection began with two pieces from quilt artist Pauline Burbidge – *Fish Dance I* and *Small Zig-Zag*, which were commissioned from and donated by Region 10 (Derbyshire, Leicestershire, Lincolnshire, Nottinghamshire and Rutland). *Bath Hanging* by Molly Taylor was purchased by the Heritage Committee, as their first contemporary acquisition, having previously concentrated solely on the acquisition of historic pieces.

As Janet Rae, Heritage Officer for The Quilters' Guild 1990–1995, explained in the Nineties Collection Catalogue: 'The Nineties Collection is one of those magical ideas that received growing support as the decade progressed'. From small beginnings at the start of the nineties, the Nineties Collection entered the twenty-first century with 51 pieces, representing many different styles of quiltmaking, commissioned and chosen by the grass roots membership of The Guild. The Heritage Committee decided to commission the final piece – *Aberdeen 1* – also from Pauline Burbidge. It felt fitting to close that Collection and the decade with the opening maker.

The idea of contemporary collecting is vital to all collections, and these pieces form the heritage collection of the future. The Heritage Committee hoped future viewers 'would marvel at the creativity as much as we do today when we see an intricate piece of Victorian needlework'. This foresight and recognition of the importance of contemporary collecting is a key moment in the history of the Guild Collection, and has provided a foundation that has since been built on with a whole range of contemporary pieces and makers, adding to the variety and breadth of The Collection which currently spans over 300 years of quilt history.

Finding a Permanent Home: 2000–2009

In June 2001 the Resource Centre at Dean Clough, Halifax, was opened to house The Guild's growing collection of heritage and contemporary quilts and its extensive library, also an important educational resource. An administrative office with paid staff for The Guild had already moved to Dean Clough in 1990, but the addition of the Resource Centre consolidated The Collection and also provided a small space for exhibitions, a quilt store with roller-racking, and a study area for researchers to access the onsite collection.

With the move of The Collection came the employment of a professionally qualified curator. The Collection became a registered museum in 2001 (later known as Accreditation), fulfilling the national standard of professional care and showing commitment to providing access for the benefit of the wider public. Exhibitions at the Resource Centre were varied and changed every few months. They displayed four or five quilts at one time plus some smaller items, and opened free of charge two days per week (and other days by appointment).

New storage racks at the Resource Centre, Halifax

The Resource Centre was adequate for a short-term move, but its geographical location was not ideal, and access by public transport made visiting problematic. As The Collection kept rapidly expanding, a search for a new, permanent home was taken up by Heritage Officer Janet Rae. The challenge became a five-year search for a suitable place to both store and exhibit The Collection; to provide research and educational access; be the home for educational activities; and to centralise all the operations required for The Guild's vibrant and growing quilting community.

In the meantime, the quilt Collection continued to be exhibited at various venues across the UK including a regular slot at The Festival of Quilts which, after an initial exhibition in 1999 at Lord's Cricket Ground in London, became an annual event from 2003 at the N.E.C. in Birmingham. The Festival of Quilts provided a perfect showground for The Collection, regularly reaching tens of thousands of visitors who were already deeply interested in quilts and textiles. The Collection also had an additional benefit from The Festival of Quilts: the winner of The Quilters' Guild Challenge competition category, sponsored by Bernina, was automatically added to The Collection, providing very recent high-quality contemporary work. However, as the same artists won in consecutive

The Great Hall in St Anthony's before the Museum opened, 2008

Moving The Guild Office and Collection into St Anthony's Hall, May 2008

years, this rule was later changed to a donation of £1000 to the Acquisitions Fund by Bernina for the purchase of contemporary pieces chosen by the Collections Committee.

Within The Guild, this decade saw the establishment of three further specialist groups, to champion particular styles of quilting – Contemporary Quilt Group in 2002, Miniature Quilt Group in 2003 and Traditional Quilt Group in 2005. In 2005, The Quilters' Guild commissioned another anniversary collection to celebrate its 25th anniversary. The 25 for 25 Collection comprised 25 pieces from makers whose work was not already represented, and provided another body of contemporary work to illustrate current quiltmaking trends. 2005 also saw the publication of *The Quilters' Guild Collection: Contemporary Quilts, Heritage Inspiration* which featured work from 12 contemporary quiltmakers who were inspired by objects from the Heritage Collection, showing contemporary designs rooted in historical traditions.

The Quilt Museum and Gallery at St Anthony's Hall, York

Lilian Hedley demonstrates traditional wholecloth quilting to Janet McCallum and Pauline Burbidge

Loans to external venues continued, and in 2006, 46 items from The Collection travelled to Japan for an exhibition at The Tokyo International Quilt Festival, held at the Tokyo Dome. Japanese visitors were thrilled to see examples from British quilting heritage, and marvelled at the very British phenomenon of the quilted and patchwork tea cosies, which were, without a doubt, the most popular items in the exhibition.

In May 2008, The Quilters' Guild and its Collection moved to St Anthony's Hall, one of four medieval guildhalls in York. With the move came an expansion in staff to administer all the functions of The Guild. The recently refurbished St Anthony's had two gallery spaces, a large education room, a larger store with double the provision of roller-racking, a large quilt examination area, a library, members' room and multiple offices.

In June 2008, the Quilt Museum and Gallery was opened as Britain's first dedicated museum to the heritage of the allied crafts of patchwork, quilting and appliqué. Its opening exhibition, *Quilts in Time: Journey from Bed to Wall,* curated by renowned textile curator Helen Joseph, combined historic pieces from The Collection with contemporary works on loan from leading textile artists, showing the shift from functional domestic piece to artistic object. This was followed in October 2008 with an international exhibition *Quilting around the Globe and across the Centuries* on loan from the International Quilt Study Center, University of Nebraska, Lincoln, USA in the Great Hall, with a late Victorian themed *Patchwork for the Parlour* exhibition in the smaller Bailey Gallery.

Exhibition preview of *Quilts in Time: Journey from Bed to Wall, 2008*

The Bailey Gallery at the Quilt Museum and Gallery, June 2008

Quilt Museum Director Fiona Diaper (centre) at the opening exhibition with (left to right) Di Goodison, Kaffe Fassett and Janice Gunner

Installing the opening exhibition, *Quilts in Time; Journey from bed to wall*, curated by Helen Joseph

1718 Silk Patchwork Coverlet

Made in 1718 | 169cm x 185cm | Acquired in 2000

The 1718 Silk Patchwork Coverlet is the most iconic item in The Quilters' Guild Museum Collection, and the earliest known British patchwork with initials and a date worked into the piece. It is an important representation of the style and techniques in use in the early eighteenth century and as a dated piece it provides a benchmark for other rare surviving patchwork pieces from this period. The coverlet is a beautiful and unique design, featuring 182 blocks of both simple geometric designs and intricate figurative motifs. Worked in a rich variety of plain and woven silks, most of which were recycled from previous use, the maker has used the mosaic patchwork technique to create a true masterpiece – no other surviving silk patchwork object from the eighteenth century has such a complex design.

Purchased in 2000 at an auction in Oxfordshire for The Quilters' Guild Museum Collection, this internationally important piece of textile history has since been conserved, examined and researched by numerous experts. They have produced a large body of work exploring the origins, construction, internal papers and historical context of the piece, as well as researching possible candidates for the elusive owner of the initials E H – which also feature twice in blue silk cross stitch worked on the linen reverse of the coverlet. Although we do not know for certain who E H was, we know the piece came from the Brown family, whose ancestors were farming gentry from Aldbourne, Wiltshire. We can also make a number of assumptions based on the patchwork itself. The fabrics are good quality with a few containing metal threads, supporting the belief that the family were of good social position. Further indications of this are the leisure time needed to work on the project, the use of valuable paper for the templates, and the competent sewing skills, demonstrated by the accurate piecing and the neat 15–20 stitches per inch.

In 2004, The Quilters' Guild completed a three-year project led by Pauline Adams to produce a replica 1718 Silk Patchwork Coverlet, emulating the original as closely as possible. Each block was completed by a member of The Quilters' Guild, and the finished coverlet is also an important piece within The Collection.

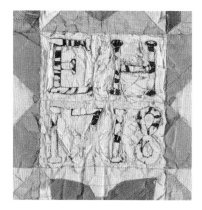

The central block featuring the initials and date 'EH 1718'

The Replica 1718 Coverlet, completed by Quilters' Guild members in 2004

Early Nineteenth-century Crib Coverlet

Made 1780–1820 | 121cm x 149cm | Acquired in 2001

This crib coverlet is made of late eighteenth and early nineteenth-century printed cottons. Despite the intention of being made for a child, this piece is highly decorative and would have been time consuming to make, with tiny squares forming the basis of alternate blocks that have all been hand-sewn together. At this time, high-quality printed cotton fabrics were expensive and treasured, and this piece really does use up the smallest of scraps. The other blocks feature squares on point, and four corner blocks showcase a mosaic patchwork flower, which has been fussy-cut to show off a floral print in the centre.

The range of early printed cottons and the tiny patchwork pieces make this coverlet both important and beautiful. Cot and crib coverlets are also quite rare. By their nature and use on children's beds they were often subject to a lot of use and potential cleaning, adding more wear to the pieces and decreasing the likelihood of their longer-term survival. Unlike other children's items which are kept for best, those practical items in daily use tend to be used to destruction.

When this piece entered The Collection its condition was very poor. Due to the age and nature of the piece, the brown fabrics had suffered a high level of deterioration, especially on the outer border, leaving the coverlet fragile and vulnerable to further decay. It had also been carelessly looked after at some point in its past, and small white paint splashes were evident over the whole surface until it was conserved in 2011.

Flower patchwork block with fussy-cut pieces

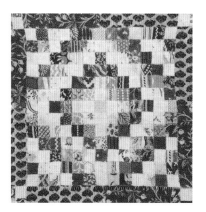

Tiny squares arranged to form light and dark diamonds

Blue and Gold Welsh Strippy Quilt

Made 1900–1920 | 195cm x 213cm | Acquired in 2002

Made from stripes of blue and gold fabric, this is a bold and striking traditional Welsh strippy quilt, with hand-quilted motifs of fans, wheels and church windows with three spirals sewn in red thread. Unlike the North Country-style strippy, whose quilting motifs usually follow the front patchwork strips forming rows of quilting designs, this quilt's overall design still follows the traditional Welsh framed layout that is used on both strippy and wholecloth pieces. This is probably one of the heaviest pieces in The Collection, and the thick wool or blanket wadding means that the stitches are not as close or as neat as lighter wholecloth examples.

Quiltmaking in Wales was often a professional occupation and was one of the few ways a woman could earn a living. The professional Welsh quilter would travel from household to household, either on their own or with an apprentice, making quilts to order for local housewives. The customer would normally provide all materials, food and lodgings for the quilters, who would then board with them for the duration of the quiltmaking. This annual visit to households, and quilting in general, began to decline by the early twentieth century, as the introduction of cheap mass manufactured alternatives such as 'comfy' quilts, eiderdowns and bedspreads threatened the traditional craft. Quilters found it increasingly difficult to earn a decent wage for the effort involved. By the end of the First World War, many younger women had moved away to cities and towns to help with the war effort and were less willing to learn a craft that was considered time consuming with little reward.

This quilt is one of 20 donated to The Guild as part of the Angela Brocklebank Bequest. The other pieces include pieced designs, strippies, frame quilts and wholecloths, and as a collection represent good-quality but fairly ordinary, everyday pieces from the nineteenth and early twentieth centuries. Angela was a proud Guild supporter and was well known for her vibrant character. She was an avid collector of quilts and an enthusiastic quilt historian, and travelled extensively to assist with the British Quilt Heritage Project during the 1990s.

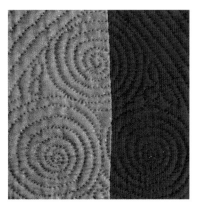

Welsh spiral motif

Central circular medallion

Hearts and Crosses Coverlet

Made 1875–1900 | 187cm x 214cm | Acquired in 2003

The scrappy nature and folk charm of this piece makes it instantly likeable, and it is often a visitor favourite when exhibited. Made from strips of roller-printed cottons in various colours and designs, the coverlet's layout uses bold and striking borders of Turkey red fabric with appliquéd white hearts arranged in clusters of two and four. The central diamond of the coverlet contains appliqué crosses. It is unknown whether the hearts and crosses have any particular significance to the maker, or if they just used popular motifs to add further decoration to the coverlet.

Hearts and Crosses appliqué detail

In many ways there is nothing particularly spectacular about this piece. Late Victorian cotton patchworks were still quite common, though most probably from women lower down the social scale as more fashionable ladies would have preferred the use of silks and velvets. The construction is quite simple, and it was probably machine sewn for speed of completion. Yet the fact that it is quite ordinary is what makes it worthy of collecting. Many items of textiles in museum collections are treasured and saved because they are atypical of those in everyday use – the special, the sentimental, the 'too good to use'. Documenting the everyday fabrics and the ordinary pieces is just as important, and more representative of what was actually being used at the time.

Organic Radiation by Kaffe Fassett

The design and arrangement of the stripes in this coverlet is also quite unique to the maker, and certainly inspired Kaffe Fassett to create his own version after first viewing it in 2003 and again for his exhibition *Ancestral Gifts* at the Quilt Museum and Gallery in 2015; it also featured in the publication *Heritage Quilts* that accompanied the exhibition. That later reincarnation, entitled *Organic Radiation*, encapsulates the feel of the original, with the same dynamic stripes radiating from the centre. Some of the larger-scale floral prints present in the original were emphasised in the centre and outer border of Kaffe's version. *Organic Radiation* was kindly donated by Kaffe for The Collection in 2018.

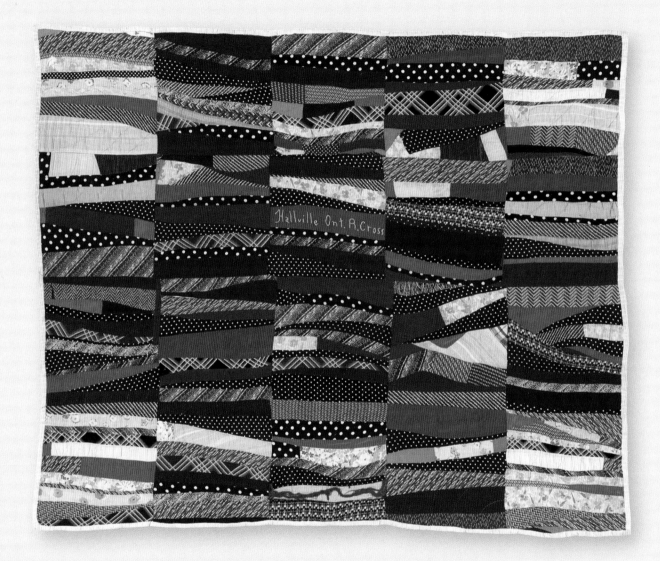

Hallville Canadian Red Cross Quilt

Made in the 1940s | 185cm x 152cm | Acquired in 2003

Whilst our collecting policy clearly states that all items must be of British origin, the inclusion of some non-British pieces in The Collection is permissible if the piece represents a style or historical event that had an impact on British patchwork and quilting history. This Canadian Red Cross quilt is made from five vertical strips pieced together, with each made up from horizontal strips of different dress fabrics in a mixture of designs including spots, stripes and floral designs. The cotton backing still has the original Red Cross label, which was sometimes removed from these quilts by the recipient who didn't want to be associated with receiving charity. Makers of these quilts were not allowed to write their names on the quilts, as these were considered gifts from Canada to Britain rather than from individuals, but occasionally some details, such as the name of the town, were included as part of the design. The central strip shows this piece was made in Hallville, Ontario.

An extensive number of Canadian Red Cross quilts were made and sent across for the care and comfort of British families, patients and service people during the First and Second World Wars. These quilts were often produced quickly with any materials readily to hand, and groups often worked to produce blocks individually which could then be quickly joined together, finished and sent overseas. The utilitarian nature of these pieces meant that crazy patchwork, where any shape, design and size of fabric can be utilised, was a popular choice, but there is in fact a great deal of variety in surviving examples. This piece is nicely designed and neatly sewn, showing a range of dress and blouse fabrics from the thirties and forties.

It was given to the family of Bill Richards, whose house in Bexley was hit by a doodlebug in 1944 whilst the family were on holiday in Devon with their neighbours. He remembers staying with his grandparents until the family were able to return to their home in 1945, which is when they received the Red Cross parcel that contained this quilt. He also remembers using this quilt for years afterwards on both his, and his children's bed.

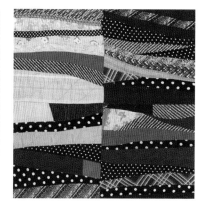

Some horizontal strips were joined from several pieces

Embroidered text showing where the piece was made

The Bloomfield Coverlet

Made in 1850 | 230cm x 246cm | Acquired in 2004

The design of this mid-Victorian coverlet is very unusual, and its importance in The Collection is partly due to its relationship with a 'sister' coverlet that is closely linked by design, fabrics and family ties. The design features appliquéd hexagon clusters and squares of cross-stitched religious text with printed cotton borders. The central design has a dedication to 'Edwin. Mary Bloomfield 1850', the recipients and owners of the coverlet. Family history records show that Edwin Bloomfield married Mary Newson in 1827, and had 11 children, 9 of whom made it to adulthood. As a local magistrate in an extensive family home in Great Glemham, Suffolk, the family employed five domestic servants and lived a very comfortable lifestyle. As several of the religious passages relate to the death of children it has often been thought that this coverlet also serves a commemorative purpose for its recipients, honouring two children lost in childhood.

Closely connected with this piece is the Wyatt Coverlet, which features the same text boxes and Maltese cross designs found on the Bloomfield – and in fact some of the same fabric. Acquired at slightly different times, it was clear these pieces were related. An appeal in *The Quilter* magazine raised the money for the purchase of the second piece. Researchers into both coverlets found that Reverend William Wyatt's wife – Anne Newson – was Mary's sister. Dated the year before, 1849, the Wyatt Coverlet has a border of older fabric which was most probably recycled from a previous use. In contrast, as the second project the Bloomfield Coverlet features a fashionable contemporary swagged tassel print design.

The similarities between the coverlets, and the known family connection of sisters Anne and Mary Newson, are interesting – but we still don't know exactly who made the patchworks. Their position in society, and William Wyatt's connection as chaplain of the Nottingham lunatic asylum, has led some to suggest these coverlets were therapeutic projects made by inmates and dedicated to these families as benefactors in the community. We'll never really know the full story behind the creation of these two fascinating pieces, but they are certainly both unusual coverlets with unique stories to tell.

Edwin and Mary Bloomfield's names feature in the very centre

Cross-stitched text in red leaf border

Kaleidoscope, Alicia Merrett

Up the Stairs, Elizabeth Brimelow

Singing in the Rain, Jo Rednall

They Cast a Spell on Me, Laura Kemshall

The 25 for 25 Collection

In celebration of its 25th anniversary, The Quilters' Guild decided to follow on from the success of the Nineties Collection and to commission a new set of 25 quilts to represent the creativity of contemporary quiltmakers whose work was not already present in The Collection, aiming to showcase the best of early twenty-first-century work.

As before, the Guild Regions commissioned the majority of the works, with two further commissions by the Acquisitions Committee and the last piece being the winner of an open challenge at The Festival of Quilts in 2004.

The quilts, which each measure no larger than 1 metre square, represent a wide range of styles, techniques and subject matter. Whilst they are contemporary in nature, the traditional techniques still underpinned all the works. Janice Gunner, president of The Guild between 2005 and 2008, wrote in the catalogue that traditional techniques had just been 'used in other ways – moved on, adapted or manipulated to fit in with the many new ways of expressing the medium of the quilt'. The catalogue was kindly sponsored by Bernina UK, whose continued support in the area of contemporary quilts for The Collection can be found in their generous sponsorship of The Quilters' Guild Challenge at The Festival of Quilts, and later a regular donation to the Acquisitions Fund for the purpose of purchasing contemporary works.

Scott Log Cabin

Made in 1860 | 179cm x 182cm | Acquired in 2005

Log cabin is a versatile patchwork technique and became popular in the second half of the nineteenth century stitched with both printed cottons and more expensive velvets and silks. The strips of fabric are arranged in light and dark shades around a central square, and blocks are combined in a vast array of layouts that create additional patterns in the overall design. The design of this piece arranges the log cabin blocks to form concentric diamonds of light and shade, creating a striking visual design, and it has been made from printed cottons with red and black polka-dot centres. The coverlet is backed in Turkey red paisley print cotton and has a frill on all four sides made from the same fabric.

The coverlet was made by Elizabeth Scott of Selkirk for her daughter, Martha Hogg, in 1860. Martha married a tailor, who was distantly related to James Hogg, the 'Ettrick Shepherd', who is now recognised as an important Scottish writer and poet, and who had a close relationship with Sir Walter Scott. However, its distant relation to celebrity poets is not what has marked it as a significant log cabin piece.

With a date of 1860, it is probably the earliest log cabin in The Collection, and one of the earlier pieces made using this block, which remained in popular use until the early twentieth century. The exact origins and development of the block are unknown, but more references to it are found later in the nineteenth century, making this piece one of the earlier uses of the block. It's also very striking, especially when viewed vertically, although it is likely the maker would never have expected to have seen it hanging on a wall.

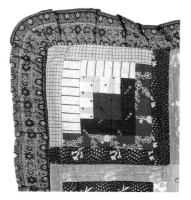

Turkey red paisley print frill

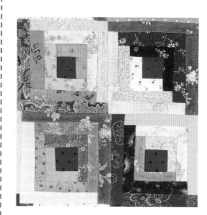

Detail of log cabin blocks

Kent Uniform Coverlet

Made 1860–1880 | 209cm x 211cm | Acquired in 2005

The design and heavy woollen fabrics of this uniform coverlet represent a different style of patchwork. Sometimes known as soldiers' coverlets or military coverlets, these pieces use colourful uniform fabrics in often complex geometric designs, and the cumbersome thickness of the fabrics meant they were made by men rather than women. Sometimes they were men serving in the armed forces; other makers were tailors who had access to the offcuts from uniform making. Either way, it is not the usual female creator who makes up the lion's share of our maker profile.

That's not to say we don't have other pieces in The Collection made by men, and some of the pieces that have undocumented provenance could also be from male makers. Several quilts and coverlets have been made by tailors, and use suiting samples and offcuts, making pieces dark in colour and masculine in tone. But care must be taken not to stereotype. A predominantly pink floral and animal print cotton patchwork from the 1870s covered with colourful braid was made by an Indian army officer and later policeman; and Ray Marshall, a renowned potter from the 1970s, used a wealth of vibrantly coloured printed cottons in his strippy blocks quilt.

The colourful nature of these pieces shows that soldiers' uniforms were not the camouflaged shades we associate with the military today. And of course uniforms themselves were made for other domestic purposes, such as household livery and hunting, as well as for military ceremonial purposes. Different contrast colours for military uniforms were also used on facings of the uniforms, accounting for the large range of colours in these uniform pieces.

The central medallion shows off a decorative and beautifully executed floral design

Blue wool fringing edges the whole piece

69

Field Force

Made in 1996 by Michele Walker | 300cm x 200cm | Acquired 2006

The traditional style of North Country wholecloth quilting takes on a new dimension in this piece by Michele Walker, whose work often deals with challenging the conventional associations of a 'quilt'. Her work is frequently inspired by personal experiences and observations from the world around her, and this particular piece uses a unique tyre-tread quilting pattern that represents the tyres making their mark on the landscape of the South Downs near Walker's home. This destruction of the natural habitat is further emphasised by the use of household plastic bags that form the top layer of the quilt. Although the techniques are the same, this quilt is not the usual quilt, conveying warmth and comfort; but rather a stark and harsh wake-up call for the environmental problems we face in the twenty-first century.

This piece represents an important acquisition for The Collection, placing emphasis on large contemporary works that use the medium of quilting as an artistic form to express social and political issues. She combines traditional techniques with non-conventional materials in the firm belief that whilst her work takes inspiration from historical quilting techniques, it still reflects the time in which it was made.

Michele had an instrumental role as a founder member of The Guild and was the officer in charge of exhibitions in the initial steering committee. She is an author, contemporary practitioner, researcher, artist and curator, and explores the quilting works and traditions of other cultures: she received an Arts and Humanities grant in 2003 to explore Japanese sashiko works. This particular piece was purchased in 2006 with funds raised from the Margaret Tucker Memorial Fund, which was donated to by members in memory of another founder member, a former Guild Trustee and keen supporter of The Quilters' Guild.

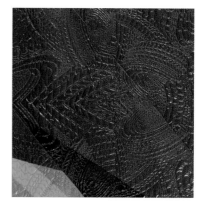

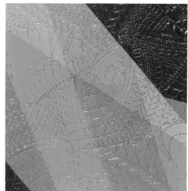

Details of tyre track quilting motifs

Turmoil and Change

Made in 2005 by Diana Harrison | 126cm x 137cm | Acquired in 2007

This contemporary silk quilt has been pieced and then distorted by stitching, and overprinted with metallic pigments. The artist's studio practice is concerned with visual and tactile qualities resulting from complex manipulations of cloth. This piece represents a period of change in the artist's creative working, and also conveys a sense of energy and excitement that occurs when an artist explores a new direction.

Whilst creating this piece, the artist was experimenting with continual stitching, trying to avoid starting and stopping, creating a great feeling of movement and flow within the stitched lines of the piece. This stitched movement was symbolic of what the artist described as her 'endless commute' of roads and roundabouts between her home in London and work at the University of Creative Arts in Farnham. The title *Turmoil and Change* referred to a new course leader for the textile department where Harrison had taught for years; she had a vision and lots of energy, which stirred things up!

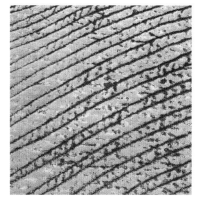

Detail of stitched lines and painted surface

Stitching lines create a sense of movement

Pink Boat (Dry Dock)

Made in 1988 by Jo Budd | 292cm x 189cm | Acquired in 2009

This large contemporary pictoral quilt could almost be described as a painting with fabrics, and its style and construction sets it apart from many of the other contemporary and artistic pieces in The Collection. It was inspired by a boat in dry dock awaiting painting. The textured rusty surface, patinated markings and abstract patterns caused by circular sanding down through the many layers of paint all captivated the artist, who sought to balance the abstract qualities of the piece with enough suggestions of a three-dimensional, accessible subject, by reproducing the way the light played on the rounded belly of the boat and the contrast of the precise outline of the portholes.

The quilt is constructed with a backing canvas, overlaid with pieced and collaged Procion-dyed silk and cotton, and pigment-dyed Viyella and cotton. The surface has then been further embellished with partial overlays of re-used chiffon scarves and pigment-dyed nylon net. Some of the overlaid fabrics have been attached using a fusible web. The quilt has been free machine quilted with two shades of nylon thread – dark and transparent.

This piece was the first of a nautical structure series that marks a key step forward in the artist's practice and demonstrates considerable complexity in both the image portrayed and the techniques and materials involved in achieving this abstract yet accessible design. Michele Walker described Budd as having 'the vision of a painter with the approach of a traditional quiltmaker', and certainly the amalgamation of the two are very apparent in her work, which is now represented in many public and private collections. This piece was purchased in 2009 with assistance from the Art Fund and the V&A/MLA purchase grant.

Detail of surface embellishment

The artist, Jo Budd, in front of the piece

A Museum and Beyond: 2010–2019

The first half of this decade was a busy time as exhibitions at the Quilt Museum and Gallery changed three times a year to showcase The Collection. The Museum steadily attracted around 12 000 visitors a year and hosted both heritage and contemporary exhibitions at the same time to satisfy the variety of visitors' preferences.

The most popular exhibition, by a large margin, was Kaffe Fassett's *Ancestral Gifts*, which exhibited 15 historic quilts from The Collection, chosen by Kaffe, displayed side by side with his own inspired re-interpretations, attracting 8914 visitors in the summer of 2015. This exhibition went on to tour three venues in the USA, reaching further international audiences at the Houston International Quilt Festival, The Museum of Quilts and Textiles in San Jose, and the Michener Art Museum in Doylestown, Pennsylvania. *Sewing in Wartime* attracted the second largest number of visitors (5368) in the summer of 2010, and displayed a mix of Canadian Red Cross quilts and other wartime pieces from The Quilters' Guild Museum Collection

Setting the Scene exhibition, 2014

and loaned quilts from the personal collections of members of the Canadian Red Cross Quilt Research Group. In third place was *Setting the Scene* in Summer 2014 – a combination of period costumes from film and television on loan from Cosprop complemented by quilts and patchwork from the same period, which attracted 5247 people.

The existence of the museum helped to raise further the profile of The Guild and its Collection, and both donations and purchases increased the size of The Collection to its current number of just over 850 objects. In purely numerical terms, fewer items were accepted in the fourth decade than in the two previous decades. However, the number of items offered was greater than those accepted, and with such an extensive dedicated collection already in existence, the challenge for the Collections Committee was (and still is) to remain conscious of available storage space and resources, avoid duplication, and look for items that fill a gap in the historical timeline. The Collections policy was refocused several times as the decade progressed to recognise areas of strength and weakness, outline areas for expansion, and reassess what was under-represented. At the most recent reassessment it was clear that there were a few areas missing from our current holdings, including work representing community projects linked to social activities, works by notable makers and teachers from the last 30

Ancestral Gifts exhibition, 2015 by Kaffe Fassett
© Tony Bartholomew

The decision to close the Museum in October 2015 was a difficult one to make, but its future was financially unsustainable. Whilst the decision was disappointing, The Quilters' Guild had a lot to be proud about. In seven years the Museum welcomed more than 92 000 people to over 50 exhibitions, as well as teaching sewing skills to around 8000 children through its education activities. Visitor numbers were high for such a specialist collection, and these years represent an important chapter in the history of The Collection.

years, and significant examples continuing traditional and regional forms of patchwork and quilting from the mid-twentieth century onwards.

The Collection was used as the primary focus for several publications during this decade, in addition to catalogues produced in conjunction with exhibitions that featured at the Quilt Museum and Gallery and The Festival of Quilts. In 2011 a Shire publication *Patchwork and Quilting in Britain* provided a 300-year historical summary of the development of the crafts, which was illustrated by items from The Collection. In 2014 *The 1718 Coverlet* by Susan Briscoe provided an in-depth analysis of the original coverlet containing high-resolution photography of each block and full-scale patterns to enable readers to reproduce their own version of The Collection's most iconic piece. 2014 also saw the establishment of the Modern Quilt Group, the most recent of the specialist groups to be established within The Quilters' Guild. In 2019 The Collection acquired two modern quilts to ensure that this newly recognised category of quilt styles was represented.

Quilt Art: Dialogues, the last exhibition at the Quilt Museum and Gallery in 2015

A visitor admires eighteenth-century patchwork chair-seat covers in the *Tercentennial* exhibition at The Festival of Quilts 2018

Life beyond the Museum continued to provide activity for The Collection, which was still added to, loaned and exhibited, albeit in a revised format. Instead of the focus being on exhibitions at St Anthony's, working collaboratively and exhibiting The Collection in other museum and gallery venues across the country became the new working model. From 2016 to 2018 exhibitions ranging from Torquay, Llangollen, Bath, Rutland and North Yorkshire to Edinburgh, Kingussie and Wick provided a wide geographical spread for visitors to attend. Onsite access in the form of group visits and talks continued, and from 2018 onwards mini exhibitions and themed open days provide opportunities to see The Collection in its usual home in York.

The Festival of Quilts remains a significant opportunity to showcase The Collection, and a larger exhibition space from 2016 provided visitors with a high-quality museum-style curated exhibition and access to good-quality Collection items – contrasting the usual contemporary works on display elsewhere with some historical alternatives, so adding an extra dimension

to the visitor experience. In 2018 The 1718 Silk Patchwork Coverlet celebrated its 300th anniversary with an extensively researched interpretation gallery and its own dedicated space. With constant queues to see the coverlet from start to finish of the show each day, it had the maximum visitor exposure possible in just four days, providing access to 25 000 people before being taken back for a long rest in storage to ensure its preservation.

And what about future directions? The Forties Collection, the third commissioned anniversary contemporary collection, is well underway, and after an initial exhibition in a *Spotlight @ Forty* gallery at The Festival of Quilts 2019 they enter The Collection as a recent snapshot of work being produced 40 years after the formation of The Quilters' Guild.

Moving forward, The Guild is exploring more ways to provide engagement with The Collection. The recent commercial outputs that have been inspired by Collection items has raised awareness and reached those who would not have previously

Visitors have a rare chance to see the iconic and internationally significant 1718 Silk Patchwork Coverlet

Tercentennial: exhibition at The Festival of Quilts 2018

interacted with The Collection. Two reproduction fabric lines with Marcus Fabrics, inspired by the Mariner's Compass Coverlet, have provided period-accurate designs as well as raising the profile of The Collection. In a commercially driven world where funding sources are low, it is important to tap into the unique opportunities to create income as well as interpret and preserve objects from the past. Changes in technology and the potential of digital access also present great opportunities for interaction without requiring visitors to travel to see original objects or risking damage to those that are too fragile to display.

But of course, there is nothing like experiencing the real thing, and as The Collection moves into its fifth decade, The Guild is aware of the delicate balancing act required to look after the objects In its care whilst also creating opportunities for people to see our quilts in person. Since the closure of the Museum, great effort has been made to ensure that The Collection remains accessible, and we continue

to take our pieces out to the public through our collaborative approach with other museums and the events company Upper Street Events. We look to innovate by utilising social media, and over 75 000 people annually access our Collection. The Collection will continue to thrive thanks to its supporters, donors, fundraisers, sponsors and champions, who all realise the importance of such a valuable resource of social and domestic history.

Marcus Fabrics printed cottons and a compass panel inspired by the Mariner's Compass Coverlet

Sidmouth Quilt

Made 1820–1840 | 234cm x 255cm | Acquired in 2010

This quilt has a wonderful combination of features that make it an important acquisition for The Collection – the fabrics, the central panel, the quilting design, and with some provenance. The large squares of patchwork that make up the frames of this piece show the great variety of prints and vibrant colours available in the first half of the nineteenth century, and the slightly larger than normal pieces give us a really good idea of the design and pattern repeats, which we don't always get with smaller patchworks. The central block-printed panel shows a bird feeding its young in a nest. Such panels were fashionable in the 1810s and 1820s and were manufactured with the distinct purpose of being used in domestic projects such as quilts, coverlets, chair-backs, cushions and other household furnishings. This particular design must have been popular, as it is present in several quilts in other museum collections, and also as an unused panel in our own fabric collection.

Central block printed panel in the centre of the Sidmouth Quilt

The quilting design is also complex and beautiful, and provides a good example of an early, non-standardised design entirely of the maker's choosing, before traditional quilting designs and motifs became more geographically segregated into those motifs popularly used in the North Country and Wales. Following a framed format with a circular medallion centre, this fascinating design is not discernible from the front as the eye is drawn to the variety of printed cotton squares. The layout also does not follow the pattern of the patchwork, which adds to the difficulties in viewing the quilting design.

The same block printed panel, unused, in the fabric collection

The Sidmouth Quilt is so named as it was the town where the quilt had been kept – and it was presumed made by descendants of the Lake family. The exact maker of the quilt is difficult to ascertain from the family history records, but one possible candidate is Mary Letton, wife of a John Letton, a master mariner whom she married in the 1810s. However, by 1841 Mary was a pauper washerwoman living on parish relief, and her daughters were in domestic service. It is possible that this piece, which indicates some signs of a comfortable existence, was made before the family fell on harder times, possibly before the death of John Letton which left Mary a widow with no income.

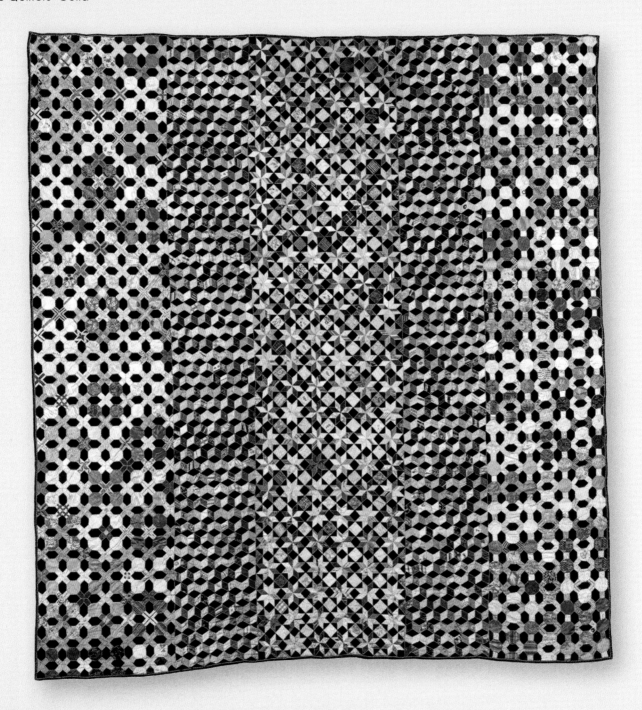

Ridehalgh Quilt

Made 1860–1890 | 205cm x 210cm | Acquired in 2011

This beautiful and intricate mosaic patchwork is made from rich silk, brocade and velvet, and each individual piece has been outlined in gold silk braid. The small pieces have been hand-sewn over paper templates, making the construction of this elaborate quilt very time consuming. It is backed with a paisley-design cotton and red wool reverse which has been quilted in a chevron design to a central cotton wadding.

The quilt was made for Colonel George John Miller Ridehalgh and his wife, of Fell Foot House in the Lake District, by their female servants, supposedly from old gowns of the lady of the house. Fell Foot, bought by Col Ridehalgh shortly after his first marriage in 1856, was a grand house with an aviary, stables and an extensive 18 acres of landscaped grounds on the east shore of Lake Windermere. The couple had at least six servants according to the 1871 census: a cook, lady's maid, housemaid, under-housemaid, kitchen maid and under-gardener. Fanny died in the early 1870s, and George remarried, but there were no children from either marriage. With no direct heirs to the Ridehalgh estate, it was passed on to the next of kin. The house was sold and eventually demolished in 1910.

A story which appeared in local papers in 2006 adds another interesting dimension to the Ridehalgh Quilt. In a secret compartment of a writing desk, a furniture restorer in Staveley found a bundle of love letters between the Colonel and his first wife, Frances (Fanny) Rosa Reade, revealing three years of courtship before their marriage in 1856. Despite remarrying, George chose to be buried with his first wife in St Mary's Church in Staveley on his death in 1892. We cannot be certain which lady of the house the quilt was made for, as this style of patchwork was popular in both women's time at Fell Foot.

The quilt was in poor condition when it was first acquired for The Collection and underwent conservation in 2013 thanks to generous donations from members of The Quilters' Guild.

Detail of star patchwork panel

Each shape was outlined in fine gold braid

83

Challans Coverlet

Made in 1811 | 215cm x 230cm | Acquired in 2012

Many of our printed cotton pieces from the early nineteenth century show the beauty and splendour of meticulous mosaic patchwork, which are a testament to the skill of their makers and indicative of their higher social status. The Challans Coverlet is a wonderful contrast to those and serves as a reminder that everyone made patchwork according to the fabrics, skills, time and education available to them. Decidedly more makeshift and hastily constructed, this piece looks like a coverlet made by someone who had a vision – and the design is certainly attractive – but didn't necessarily know how to do it. The design, appliqué method of construction and less elegant stitching all point to great enthusiasm, but little knowledge of patchwork technique.

The central medallion motif is cut out and applied onto a foundation backing. The fabric left over from cutting the leaf shapes that form the central flower also features in the corners of the centre square, the missing petal shapes showing the backing fabric behind. Frames of triangles and zigzags surround the centre, also appliquéd, but the sizes and shapes are irregular, and where the fabric has disintegrated, large stitches can be seen which contrast starkly with the tiny overstitching of more finely made mosaic pieces.

The fabric itself also indicates a poorer household, comprising cheap indigo prints that by this time were often sold from under the counter of haberdashery shops so as not to offend the richer, more fashionable clientele. The name 's. challans 1811' is nicely embroidered in cross stitch in the centre, and perhaps demonstrates that the maker's education included some sewing skills even if it did not extent to larger-scale textiles. Whilst not the best coverlet in terms of execution and quality of materials, this piece is vital in exemplifying a cross-section of makers, and in many ways is almost more important as it represents the lower classes whose textiles rarely survive in museum collections because they are more practical, need to be used, and are often used to destruction.

Central design – simple but visually effective

Embroidered name and date, presumed to be the maker's signature 's challans 1811'

Mosaic Patchwork Huswif

Made in 1856 | 11.5cm x 58cm | Acquired in 2012

This charming mosaic patchwork huswif, sometimes called a hussif or housewife, is a wonderful example of the different domestic objects that used patchwork and quilting as decoration. Intended for the storage of sewing equipment, these useful holders contained multiple pockets to keep small items separate and were also handy for travelling as they could be rolled up and tied when in transit, keeping everything conveniently in place. This particular example is unusual for its decorative diamonds design and its embroidered dedication to the intended recipient of the piece. It is also slightly out of time. Huswifs were more common in the eighteenth century, often kept in tie-on pockets which also went out of fashion with the emergence of the slimmer Regency silhouette.

The mosaic patchwork diamonds have been pieced together from roller-printed dress cottons from the 1840s and 1850s and edged with a vibrant blue silk which also decorates the pointed serrated edges of the pockets. The semicircles of felted wool fabric intended for needle storage look like uniform material and show signs of moth damage at some point in the object's past. The fabrics are quite grubby and colours have faded, but certain areas that have been less exposed show that the pinks and purples were originally much brighter.

The cross-stitched dedication 'A gift from Sarah Iles to Edward Buckler 1856' gives us a maker, recipient and date, and tell us this was made as a gift, perhaps for a specific occasion. A location would have been useful (sadly not included), but initial research did yield a few speculative results. A male recipient is more unusual and could have indicated a profession where portable sewing kits were useful or standard issue, such as a sailor or member of the armed forces. There was an Edward Buckler born in Poolo, Dorset in 1822, who was awarded a Mate's Certificate of Service in 1855 for 22 years in the Merchant Navy on both coastal and foreign trades. So far it hasn't been possible to verify the relationship between Edward and Sarah Iles but she could have made this as a gift to commemorate his service around this time.

Cross-stitched dedication showing that the huswif was made for a man

Layered circles of felted wool intended to hold needles

Patchwork Bikini

Made in 1970 by Jean Amsden | Top: 34cm x 25cm
Bottom: 33cm x 26cm | Acquired in 2013

There are not many establishments that can boast of having a patchwork bikini in their collection, and this certainly stands as one of the more unusual pieces amongst our other costume items. It was made in 1970 by Jean Amsden for a competition run by Sanderson, a furnishing fabric manufacturer, and was exhibited as part of the Women's Institute Exhibition at Sanderson House in June of that year. The intention was to show the variety of items that could be made using patchwork, and not conventionally what was associated with the craft or the WI – but mission accomplished! It captured the attention of the press, including the *West Sussex Gazette* and the *Daily Mirror*, which ran the headline 'It's the itsy bitsy teeny weeny Women's Institute bikini' on 30 May 1970.

The construction of the bikini is the traditional mosaic patchwork method, and the heavy Sanderson furnishing fabrics are perhaps not ideal for the purpose. However, as a showpiece rather than practical beachwear the designs, especially the placement of the bikini-top flowers, were thoughtfully arranged. The bikini was further featured in the publication *Creative Patchwork* by June Field in 1974, and as a head-turner and advocate for the variety of applications of patchwork it certainly did its job.

Detail of Sanderson fabric designs

Karen Kerr modelled the bikini for the *Daily Mirror* in 1970
© Mirrorpix

Red Manor House Coverlet

Made in the 1850s | 249cm x 256cm | Acquired in 2013

The charming central red manor house and the vast array of flower and animal motifs caught the imaginations and hearts of Quilters' Guild members when this large appliqué coverlet came up for auction in 2013. Appliqué is often rarer than patchwork and quilting, and this is an extensive example, showcasing each motif in its own square block which is then surrounded by colourful printed cotton sashing. The subjects of each block are distinctly ordinary in nature, and the rural animals and potted plants are probably a reflection of what the maker saw around her. In this way it has interesting links to the motif designs in the 1718 Silk Patchwork Coverlet.

Sadly, we know nothing for certain about the maker, and only part of its life and travels which occurred after its creation. We know from the auction information that it was purchased in 1971 for £28. When the coverlet was documented at the London British Quilt Heritage Project Documentation Day in 1993, it was recorded that the family travelled from Gloucestershire to South Africa, taking the coverlet with them, but later returned to live in Princes Risborough in Buckinghamshire. As the coverlet was already made at the time of the family's travels, we know the design must have been inspired by their previous home. Whilst we don't have specific family information, we can assume the maker was middle class, and had access to fabrics, time and sewing skills. Whilst some of the designs are more naïve in style than others, they are carefully thought out and each piece has herringbone stitch around the edge, a time-consuming addition. The large size of the piece could indicate a reasonable-sized bed and therefore a comfortable household.

The coverlet was the inspiration for a Block of the Month project launched by The Quilters' Guild at The Festival of Quilts in 2019 to celebrate the 40th Anniversary of The Guild. The red house at the centre of the piece was perfect for the Ruby anniversary, and the block-like construction and inclusion of houses links back to the very first acquisition into The Collection 40 years ago – The House Blocks Quilt.

Detail of the cow and heart block

Detail of the horse block

Mosaic Patchwork Chair-seat Covers

Made 1730–1750 | 44.5cm x 35cm | Acquired in 2014

Surviving patchwork from the first half of the eighteenth century is rare. The Guild acquired six silk mosaic patchwork chair-seat covers in 2014, which filled a chronological gap between the 1718 Silk Patchwork Coverlet and the printed cotton hexagon pieces from the final decades of that century. Dating around mid-century, with some fabrics that potentially date up to 70 years before the patchwork itself was constructed, these covers show that the square block quartered into triangles was still the predominant shape used at this time.

Patchwork in the eighteenth century was a popular and fashionable activity. Jonathan Swift's *Direction to Servants in General* (1745), indicated that servants could no longer benefit from cast-off clothing due to the fashion amongst ladies for 'turning them to cover easy Chairs, or making them into Patch-work for Skreens, Cushions and the like'. Silks were the fashionable fabrics of choice at the start of the century, and these precious and expensive fabrics were saved, recycled and re-used to create colourful designs. The paper templates in these pieces remain *in situ*, providing stability to the shapes. Recycled from household documents, the papers themselves are an endless source of fascination.

Each chair-seat cover is slightly different, with all but one featuring a central patchwork star with additional embroidery and couching. There are a number of high-quality silks containing metallic threads, and one very interesting metallic woven ribbon which reads 'No popery, No slavery'. Dating from the Glorious Revolution of 1688, this phrase embodied the increasing public fear of a Catholic tyranny which reached feverish heights. At this time Charles II's daughter Mary and her Dutch husband William of Orange were urged by English peers to overthrow James II's rule which threatened to overturn previous restrictions on Catholic influence, worship and admittance to positions of power. This ribbon would have been a way of expressing Protestant support for the Revolution, a subtle and domestic expression of a huge political and religious event.

'No popery no slavery' ribbon woven in metallic thread

The paper templates in the reverse were recycled from letters, newspapers and children's handwriting practice

Honesty Skyline

Made in 2015 by Pauline Burbidge | 133cm x 164cm | Acquired in 2017

Honesty Skyline is one of Pauline Burbidge's latest pieces, made using cyanotype and mono printing techniques incorporating the plants and flowers that surround the artist's home in the Scottish Borders. Known as a Quiltscape, it is one of a series of textile landscapes whose imagery is inspired by the changing natural landscape. This particular piece uses the translucent circular seedpods of the honesty plant (*Lunaria annua*) to print onto cotton lawn and silk organza. Red hot poker leaves were used to create fabric rubbings on cotton organdie, with more designs drawn underneath using a fabric marker stick. The layers of the fabric collage have all been hand stitched and hand quilted. This piece was exhibited in the Pauline Burbidge *Quiltscapes & Quiltlines* exhibition at the Bowes Museum in 2016, which featured 22 quilts and framed stitch drawings by the artist, made between 2003 and 2015.

Pauline Burbidge is a professional quiltmaker with an impressive career. She made her first quilt in 1976 and was a founder member of The Quilters' Guild of the British Isles in 1979. She comments: 'In those early days, people would ask what I did – I would answer "I am a quiltmaker". They would immediately think I made duvets or duvet covers, then occasionally their thoughts would go towards images of traditional quilts. Then I would steer them towards a link between traditional quilts and my art school training. And slowly the words "contemporary quiltmaker" began to emerge.' Four decades on, Pauline is still creating pioneering work – constantly evolving, exploring and innovating, as one of Britain's leading quilt artists. Her work is viewed, known and sold worldwide, and features in both private and museum collections. She currently produces both studio artwork creations which take months of work; and practical, functional pieces that she describes as 'light relief' and 'speedier and fun'.

When asked about the evolution of her work, she says, 'The development and enquiry of my own visual language is constantly changing; without this change my interest wouldn't be sustained'.

Detail of the design produced by the red hot poker leaves

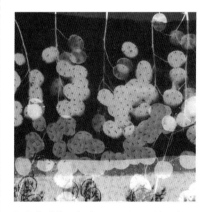

Detail of the design produced by the honesty seed pods

Corded Quilted Stomacher

Made c.1730 | 26cm x 31cm | Acquired in 2018

Surviving examples of patchwork and quilting from the early eighteenth century are rare, and this beautiful and decorative linen stomacher is an exemplary piece of craftsmanship, most likely produced by a professional quilter for a wealthy client as part of a daywear ensemble. Intricately created from corded quilting, tiny backstitches form parallel channels for the fine cord to be inserted. The floral design has been further enhanced by a combination of different embroidery stitches, French knots and pulled work within the flowers and leaves. The back of the stomacher is made from a coarser linen.

A stomacher is a piece of female clothing designed to fill in the gap between the two edges of an open robe, covering the stays underneath. These were pinned in place, and easily interchangeable, meaning they could be mixed and matched with different dresses. Quilted stomachers were often cut down from other items, but this one has been designed and made to fit the specific shape, making it much more unusual.

Both corded and flat quilting were used on a variety of different clothing items from the eighteenth century, including babies' caps, petticoats, waistcoats, nightcaps and detachable pockets. The Collection also has several babies' caps with corded quilting, a white linen man's nightcap with flat quilting worked in backstitch, and a green silk flat quilted petticoat. Patchwork and quilting were rarely found together at this time, as patchwork remained the domain of the amateur at home whilst quilting was often produced professionally in workshops and sold through commercial outlets.

Corded channels produce the floral design and vertical striped background

Variation and texture are created by different embroidery and pulled work techniques

Berlin Wall Quilt

Made in 2005 by Jean Grimshaw | 61cm x 152.5cm each piece |
Acquired in 2017

This poignant contemporary piece is full of emotion, capturing the maker's feelings about an experience that happened during her youth. Jean spent time in Germany with her penfriend whilst doing her A-level German course. During her visit in 1961, the Berlin Wall was put up, with members of her friend's family trapped on the East Berlin side of the wall. This event had a lasting impression on Jean, who continued to feel a deep connection with the city, visiting often. The quilt represents her feelings and experience of Berlin and its people, and her joy when the wall came down in 1989.

The quilt was carefully designed and features a central visual wall installation with barbed wire quilting running across all three triptych pieces. Techniques include fabric painting, appliqué, photograph transfers, quilting and embroidery. German phrases such as *Berlin Ohne Mauer* (Berlin without walls), *Keine Mauer* (No more walls) and the touching *Wir haben euch gerne auch in der Ferne* (We care about you, even though we are apart) show the heartfelt emotions felt by divided families and friends. Names on the back of the quilt commemorate all those who died trying to cross the wall.

This unique quilt voices a personal experience but in a wider context represents a major political, social and historic world event. Using textiles as a medium for political expression is a theme found in several other pieces in our Collection. In our contemporary works, textile artist Michele Walker's *Retread III* and *Field Force* both have political and environmental messages. In our historic pieces, the presence of the 'No popery, No slavery' ribbon in the eighteenth-century patchwork chair-seat covers shows a very early political alignment at a time when female political expression would not usually be expected.

Jean was a creative and versatile quilter and volunteered as Regional Coordinator and Newsletter Editor in Region 5 of The Quilters' Guild. This quilt was exhibited by Bristol Quilters and in an exhibition in Berlin.

Detail of German inscriptions and the barbed wire that runs across all three pieces

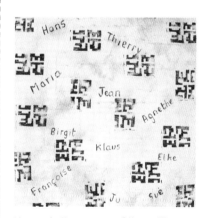

Names in the reverse of the quilt commemorate all those who died trying to cross the wall

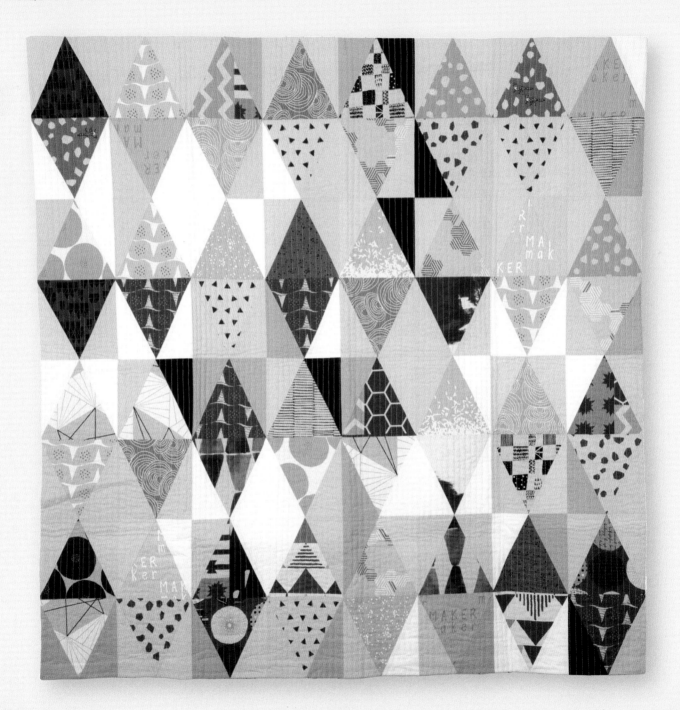

Reflections

Made in 2018 by Sarah Hibbert | 120cm x 120cm | Acquired in 2019

Reflections is a piece made in the new-style category of Modern Quilt. It was created with the intention of making the fabric prints the main attraction, and simple triangles set within squares help the viewer to focus on the beautiful and carefully chosen arrangement of Japanese prints and linen fabrics. Simple quilting enhances the design without detracting attention away from the fabric prints. This piece was one of two modern quilts accepted into The Collection at the start of 2019.

Sarah Hibbert is a Hertfordshire-based quilter, a member of Peartree Quilters and London Quilters, and joined The Quilters' Guild 31 years ago in 1988. After many years of traditional work, she became interested in modern quilts and joined the Modern Guild in the USA, visiting its major QuiltCon exhibition each year. She has had quilts accepted into the past three QuiltCon exhibitions, with an unprecedented five quilts accepted in 2019. Sarah is inspired by modern aesthetics in quilting and by the beautiful Japanese linens that she uses in her work, and she enjoys introducing a spark of colour in an odd position or twisting a block the wrong way.

Defining modern quilting is difficult; in many ways the genre can be described as a collection of stylistic and creative characteristics, not all of which need to be present to classify as a modern piece. The Modern Quilt Guild (established in 2009 in Los Angeles) defines modern quilting as 'Quilts that are functional, include bold colours and are inspired by modern design'. Elements include minimalism, asymmetry, use of negative space, and improvisational piecing. Many modern quilters use traditional blocks but give them a new twist by altering the scale or using modern printed fabric designs. It is described as an attitude and approach to quilting, which allows quilters to challenge the rules whilst respecting the artistry and traditions of its historic roots. The Guild's own Modern Quilt specialist group was formed in 2014.

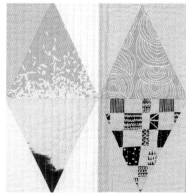

Details showing modern printed designs

Acknowledgments

The Quilters' Guild would like to thank a number of people for their help, expertise, support and advice in the making of this book.

Thanks are due to Chief Executive of The Quilters' Guild Chris Gatman; Dr Bridget Long for her historical guidance and expertise as quilt historian; members of the Collections Committee past and present; current President of The Quilters' Guild, Linda Bilsborrow; LBD Design and Katherine James for technical support; and to the generosity of all our sponsors.

A big thank you to all the curators of our Collection who have cared for it over the last 40 years: Heather Audin, Christine Brady, Tina Fenwick Smith, Mary Ranby, Danielle Sprecher, Rachel Terry, Dinah Travis and to all those who have served on the Collections Committee and the many volunteers who have contributed in large and small ways in the evolution of our Collection.

Finally, thank you to those who started with a vision in 1979 for your ideas, foresight, hard work and determination in which we can now celebrate, and all our members whose contributions and donations make all this work possible.